Focus Guru

60
Top Tips For
Terrific Time Management

"Make Every Minute Count!"

Rachael Chiverton & Jenny Leggott

"I have known Rachael through networking for many years - we have both been members of a national networking organisation, and on the voluntary teams that help to run it. In that time, Rachael has built successful meetings & teams, and is brilliant at connecting people and actually using her network. Seeing beyond the meetings as the only purpose of networking for your business is essential to get the best return on your investment. Rachael is fantastic at making sure that those she networks with get the most of their networking experience, the most out of their investment in networking, and how it can help them get focussed on their networking. These tips will be invaluable to help you get the most from your networking as they come from someone who has done exactly that herself. Rachael walks the walk."

Sheena Whyatt, KAPOW! Your Super Business Coach

"Jenny is a wonderful networker, she gets stuck into meetings as a team member, supports other groups and encourages people with things like roadtrips, turning meetings into destinations for others."

Kirsty Grimes, Love Your Biz Club

"I met Jenny through networking and I'm so glad I did. She's just one of life's most amazing people. Everyone knows that if Jenny says she's going to do something she will do it and if she can't she probably knows someone who can!"

Paul Newton, Mental Theft

"If you ever want to find someone who does XX, ask Rachael! Not only does she have a vast network, she's also always ready to help people within her network, or those new to her network, find meaningful connections."

Sian Rowsell, Sian Rowsell Coaching and Training

"Jenny's experiences and knowledge are legendary. Her ability to help others shows she fully understands the concept of how to get the best out of your time networking."

John Holden, Cabiz Networking Group & Academy

"I met Jenny through a networking event in 2020, and what struck me immediately, was how included Jenny makes everyone feel. We went on to then travel to a networking event several hours away and having those hours in the car meant I could truly absorb just how welcoming and interesting Jenny is as a person. With extensive skills in bringing people together, having asked me a few questions about myself, Jenny was immediately able to reel off names of people she felt I should connect with for business. We have become firm friends, yet Jenny still amazes me with her natural ability to bring the right people together at the right time, definitely a born networker."

NataliaValentina, Wild & Free To Be Me

"Jenny works hard to make people feel at ease as soon as you meet her. A natural networker, always looking for ways to help others and always on the lookout to pass on opportunities too. A great lady that I feel privileged to know."

Mike Turner, Greater Life

"I virtually me Rachael at an online meeting, back in 2020, during COVID. I was offered the chance to be the Group Leader of a weekly online meeting, 4N Online, Down Under, which Rachael hosted. Rachael was amazing as she put in 150% effort to ensure I succeeded. Rachael also introduced me to many other people who are now great friends. Rachael is passionate about Networking, who I highly recommend because you will not be disappointed."

Mel Jensen, Mel's Customised Candles

"I met Jenny some years ago at a 4N meeting. She was enthusiastic and helped me connect with new people to build my business."

Lesley Watts, Professional Networker

"I've known Rachael for some time and she is a brilliant networker. Rachael is always polite, informative and very welcoming."

Mel Baum, WCR Debt Collection

Focus Guru
60 Top Tips For Terrific Time Management

The moral right of Rachael Chiverton and Jenny Leggott to be identified as the authors of this work has been asserted in accordance with the Copyright, Designs and Patents Act 1988.

First published in 2023

ISBN: 9798863378282

This book is sold subject to the condition that it shall not, by way of trade or otherwise, be lent, resold, hired out or otherwise circulated in any form of binding or cover other than that in which it is published.

It is not intended to provide personalised advice and the authors disclaim any liability, loss or risk incurred as a direct or indirect consequence of the use of any contents of this work.

ABOUT THE AUTHORS

Rachael Chiverton
When not running expos and in-person networking events connecting people, Rachael helps organise people through mindset and time management. She offers online and face to face body buddy to clients who try to do it all.

www.getfocus.guru

Jenny Leggott
Alongside writing blogs, business tips and content for clients, Jenny (writing as JT Scott) has published over 50 books for children, including Sammy Rambles, Molly Manila and Bumper and Friends stories and children's activity books.

www.transcendzero.co.uk

Cover Design by Jonathan Smythe, Smooth Designs

As an award-winning art director, Jonathan helps individuals and businesses bring creative ideas to life.

www.smoothdesigns.co.uk

Contents

We all have the same 24 hours in a day

We all have the same 24 hours in a day - yet how many of your friends, family, colleagues and competitors seem to get so much more done?

Not to mention all of the people you read about in the news. How do they seem to achieve so much more in the same amount of time?

They have 24 hours in their day too.

Is it magic?

Is it luck?

It's probably a simple solution:

They are probably managing their time a little bit better than you are currently managing your time.

Don't worry! Reading this book will help you to use your time both effectively and manageably.

That's the secret of how they can be in a management meeting, do the school run, have the tidy house and tea on the table, without breaking into a sweat.

It's simple time management. It's complicated time management. It's as easy or as hard as you want it to be. You have the same 86,400 seconds in the day as everyone else.

> ➤ It's how you choose to divide up your time.
> ➤ It's how you plan how to use your time.
> ➤ It's how you do the tasks you set yourself.

It's unlikely your friend was born knowing how to manage their time perfectly. In fact there may be some days when it doesn't all go to plan.

But knowing how to use your 24 x 60 minutes in the day (yes, you can use the night hours too!) you'll find yourself achieving more in your time than ever before.

Know Why You Need Plans

There are lots of famous quotes we could share about planning, but our key advice is to pause, take a breath, and actually make a plan.

But, don't plan to plan. Try it now!

Find a pen and paper and jot down the first three things that come into your mind that need doing right now.

1. _____

2. _____

3. _____

If you need ideas, these are some examples:

➢ booking your car in for a service

➢ tidying the house before the in-laws visit

➢ making that sales call you've been putting off

➢ asking your boss for a pay rise

"Failing To Plan Is Planning To Fail"

If you KNOW what needs doing, by when, by whom, then you have a better chance of getting it done.

"Proper Planning Prevents Poor Performance"

This is WHY it's a good idea to plan. Remember to be ready to adapt if you get a curveball.

"I Don't Have Time For Planning"

This could be the reason you're reading this book.

This book will try and help YOU to make the time to do the things you really want to be doing.

"I Run Out Of Time To Get Everything Done"

This is why you NEED to pause for a moment and make a plan to use your time in the most effective way.

"Even The Best Plan In The World Won't Fix This"

Is that really true or do you just need time to make better PLANS to help achieve the tasks in your day?

Make sure there is actually enough time

It's important to be realistic with what you want to achieve and also to be realistic with the timeframe in which you want to achieve your tasks and goals.

Potentially some of your medium and long term goals will take days, weeks, months or even years to fulfil.

This is why managing your time is so important, to make sure **every minute counts**, especially with long term or complicated goals.

For example:

> ➤ Is it realistic to book a business meeting in Paris for tomorrow morning?
> ➤ Is it realistic to plan to tidy your house half an hour before your friends arrive for dinner?
> ➤ Is it realistic to do your bookkeeping while helping your children with their homework?

One of the key sources of stress with time management is not allowing enough time to manage in the first place!

Be kind to yourself too.

If you wanted to be in Paris in the morning, it might be less stressful if you had booked your ticket last month.

If your whole house needs tidying before your friends come to visit you could schedule small bursts of tidying a few days beforehand.

There's the saying that "if it wasn't for the last minute nothing would get done" and while there's some truth in that, it can be less overwhelming to divide the hours and minutes in your day in a more manageable way.

The top tip here is to make sure there is enough time to achieve the task(s) you want to do.

Make every minute count.

Use time management at home and at work

When managing your time, there's no reason why you can't use time management skills at home and at work.

In fact, learning to manage your whole day has many benefits.

You'll find you can compartmentalise "home tasks", so thinking about them doesn't take your brain power away from your work performance.

Equally, leaving some (or all) of your work worries and work plans in your office (or home office) can help you enjoy more time at home too.

In this book you'll find lots of ways to help compartmentalise your time and tasks to make the most of your day.

Encourage your family to participate

Time management isn't just your responsibility.
Time management isn't just your responsibility.
Time management isn't just your responsibility.

That's right, everyone has responsibility for managing their 24 hours in the day and their 7 days in a week.

➤ Your boss, co-workers, clients, competitors
➤ Your partner, children, pets

Everyone has some responsibility for their time and their activities, whether or not those activities cross over into your home hours or into your work hours.

You can't be responsible for how someone else spends their time. What you can do is introduce ways to share what activities and tasks need to be done, when they need doing and who needs to do them.

When everyone can see **what needs doing**, and **when it needs doing**, you might be surprised to see who steps up to do something. It might be the last person you expected to do it!

Time Management isn't limited to the workspace. Your family have time to manage too. If someone else is doing a task, it's important to give them time and space so they can complete their task.

If you don't respect someone else's time then why should they respect yours (and vice versa)?

If you can't do something or are waiting for something, are you leaving a colleague or family member in limbo?

Or are you in limbo waiting for someone else?

That's why we strongly believe time management is everyone's responsibility. You'll find once you protect your own time, others will respect your time too.

Plan ahead

We've talked a little about how planning ahead helps to make the best use of your time. Planning ahead helps you manage your time and helps towards your goals.

Is there something you can do today that might make things easier for you tomorrow?

When writing this book we asked friends and colleagues the same question. These are some of the responses:

"I fill up my car with fuel the day before going to a meeting so I don't need to do it on the day."

"I put the clothes I want to wear in the morning on a chair by my bed so I don't have to think about it when I get up. I do the same with my children's clothes and it saves so much time faffing."

"I plan meals and do an online food shop that gets delivered at the weekend so I've got enough in the cupboards for the week."

The examples here can be carried out in periods of "slow time" during the day or evening. Each task you carry out today may well save you time tomorrow.

How long have you taken today when choosing which blouse or shirt to wear?

Have you got held up in commuter traffic when you could have set off a little earlier (or later)?

The biggest time saving is in your decision making.

By becoming pro-active with your decisions you can act with clarity and purpose.

Once you've put your mind to a task it becomes much easier to complete.

What did you decide could be carried out today?

Will you do it?

Allow extra time

It might seem counterproductive when talking about time management to allow extra time for things.

Surely the idea is to make every minute count?

So, why allow extra time?

If you allow extra time to get somewhere, or allow extra time when planning something, you might feel these are wasted minutes, but **these extra minutes now can save hours in the long run**.

Jenny says, "I always try to leave a 'getting lost' buffer of 10-15 minutes when going somewhere new as I might miss a turn or end up parking further away."

Rachael says: "If you don't need the extra minutes in your schedule you'll find new opportunities arise simply from being in the right place at the right time."

For example:

> ➤ Arriving a few minutes early to networking meetings can give you the chance to talk to someone you might not have spoken with.

> ➤ Having a few minutes at the end of a meeting can give you preparation time before setting off to carry out your next task. It gives time for a coffee top-up or toilet break.

Some people say "if you're on time, you're late". They prefer to be early for everything rather than arriving exactly on time.

Unless everyone regularly synchronises their watches or phones, it's likely there will always be a minute or two difference between what time you think it is and what time someone else says it is.

Some people choose to set their watches five or ten minutes ahead. It gives them a time buffer to allow for anything unexpected to happen.

But equally having too much time ahead of your schedule can potentially absorb pockets of time you might be able to use for something else.

So the message here is to allow a reasonable amount of time for unexpected things.

For example:

> Allowing a bit of extra time if it's raining as there's likely to be extra traffic on the roads with people who usually walk or cycle taking their car instead.

> When scheduling meetings, allow a few minutes between appointments. As well as digesting the conversation you've just had and making notes for following up, you might want the toilet or a coffee, and that all takes time.

Allowing a few extra minutes in your schedule can save you hours in the long run.

Analogue, Digital or Approximate Time?

When looking at time management do you work best talking about time in digital or analogue format?

If you're a person who likes to know the exact time for things to the minute, you may prefer the precision of the digital time format.

When the numbers come up on the digital display, for example 0730, there's no debate whether it's thirty minutes past seven o'clock, or thirty-one minutes, past.

In fact, you might refer to it as "seven thirty", or "zero seven three zero local" if you're using Military Time.

In comparison, not all analogue clocks have minute markers on the clock face. This may cause ambiguity when reading the time and there's the opportunity for error when setting the time. Plus, if the clock is battery powered, time can slow down as the battery fades!

Alternatively you might be more comfortable talking about approximate times.

You might say "it's about seven-ish" or "early evening".

Unless your role depends on absolute accuracy of time there's no right or wrong way to refer to time.

It's helpful to know your own preference, especially if you're speaking with someone (at work or at home) who prefers the opposite method!

It's also worth making a brief mention that even with all of the world-time-synchronisation services, there can still be discrepancies in how each of us read the time, or even what time our phones or watches are showing.

It's not all bad news though. By being aware of our differences it can help us work together harmoniously.

Which are you?

Why does this matter?

How do your clients, colleagues, family and friends refer to time? What about speaking with people in different countries and different time zones?

Listen to your vocabulary choice as well as that of other people's when talking about time.

If you say "seven-ish" to someone who wants to be somewhere for "ten past seven" will you be in the right place at the right time?

How long would you (or they) be prepared to wait if your paths haven't crossed at the right time?

Think about train times, TV programme listings, they are given as precise times and that's helpful for knowing what's happening and at what time.

The more specific you can be with time, the more you'll be aware of what you're doing with your time and the easier it will be to manage your time and consciously be aware of how other people are using your time too.

The more aware you become of the time the more you'll be able to know what time it is without looking at a watch, clock, or phone.

You'll subconsciously pick up clues from your environment and these will help you know when it's time to move on to the next task.

Listen out for a clock chiming, or the change in light as day turns to dusk, you'll find you're more aware of the time than you think.

An example of this is if the office cleaning team always arrive at quarter to six, you might come to rely on their arrival for clearing your desk, making the last phone call or sending a message home to say you're leaving soon.

Without realising it, you've trained yourself to be aware of the time and what it signifies and this innocuous event is triggering a sequence of other events.

It's neither analogue nor digital yet intuitively you know the time of the day.

Use colours to categorise your time

While you're in the process of becoming more aware of how to manage your time, you may find it useful to start categorising tasks and activities into segments.

These segments can then be put into a logical order and you can build a picture of how your time will flow.

Examples of segments might include: eating, sleeping, work, house chores, travel etc.

Rachael says: "I recommend using different colours for the different segments. This makes it easy to see where time is being spent."

The reason behind this is simple. Having information presented in a contrast of colours attracts our eyes. This in turn makes our subconscious absorb more details.

Take this example of hanging a new picture in your living room. You'll probably notice it every day. For the first few weeks you might think, "I'm so pleased I put that picture there", or "that picture reminds me of the great time we had last year".

But, after a month you might stop noticing the picture as you carry on with daily life. It's not that the picture has gone. It's just that you've stopped seeing it.

It's exactly the same principle when you create a list in monochrome. The words are all there, but they might not catch your eye.

Our tip here is to make your home lists and work lists bright, cheerful and multicoloured so each item stands out and attracts your attention.

Rachael says: "Use brightly coloured pieces of paper, and/or multicoloured pens, to make things on your list stand out."

If you wish, you can colour co-ordinate similar items to make them stand out. You could use different colours for different family members too.

Then place your brightly coloured paper somewhere visible such as on a noticeboard or the back of a door.

Try it!

You'll soon find what works best for you.

Depending on how you're managing your time, you could use a time grid or a colour-coded spreadsheet to record activities and time spent.

With this information you can create pie charts and/or line graphs to see which tasks, people, or activities are taking up the most of your time.

Where are your time gaps?

Do you have any time thieves? Are there any surprises or are you sure you know how you're using your time?

Try this exercise with your family and colleagues - are there areas where you can swap jobs around the house or in the workplace?

➢ Would someone else be able to do a task as well (or better) than you?

➢ Could you help make someone else's job easier?

Once you can see patterns in your time you can start analysing and making changes if needed.

Do you need to allow extra time to eat a healthy meal? Or to remember to drink more water?

Do you have enough time to market your business, or to make more sales calls?

Creating a chart of your time over a day, week and month will help you know where you've allocated your time and might signpost areas you can make changes.

Avoid as many interruptions as you can

Are you good at creating a virtual protective bubble around you? If not, it's more than likely there will be times when you get interrupted.

Interruptions can be very stressful and a common source of arguments at home and at work.

> ➤ Perhaps there was a miscommunication and someone didn't understand or respect that you needed quiet time to carry out a task.

> ➤ It could be that something cropped up and needed your urgent attention.

> ➤ Maybe someone didn't respect your time and space and they just barged in.

DO NOT DISTURB

TV and radio stations have light boxes on the door that say "On Air" and people know not to come in or interrupt until the light goes out.

Would it help reduce interruptions if you had a sign saying "Do Not Disturb" or "Meeting In Progress" on the outside of your office door?

If the interruptions are mainly at home, it should be possible to say to your family you want to watch TV for an hour without interruptions, or you're phoning your friend, taking a bath or catching up on emails and don't want to be disturbed for a while.

Having **clear communication** with those around you helps everyone know what's going on.

If you have a shared work or family calendar, use it! Block out time in the calendar, either with a description of what you're doing or just blank out the time.

Anything you can do to help others know when you're available, and when you're not, will reduce interruptions!

Get organised for better concentration

It's amazing how much time you can gain when things are in the right place at the right time.

Making time to tidy up your desk, workspace, kitchen, car or living space saves lots of time in the long run.

It's up to you whether you tidy up as you go or have a mega tidy-up or decluttering session once a month.

Decluttering can be therapeutic!

Coming into work with a tidy office should free your mind to be creative and give yourself thinking space to come up with new ways to achieve things.

If you're wading through dumped paperwork, empty crisp packets or dozens of sticky notes just to get to your keyboard, then subconsciously, your mind is revisiting these items too.

How many times have you heard the saying:

"Tidy Desk = Tidy Mind"

Maybe when you were growing up your home was super-clean or super-messy and you've carried this with you into later life.

It's time to let go!

Create your own optimum productive zone.

If you feel inspired each time you sit or stand at your workspace that's great. If you don't feel inspired and raring to go then it's time to make some changes!

You'll find you can take small steps to help to maximise your concentration levels simply by tidying and decluttering your living, working and travel space.

Free up your energy for important tasks and goals.

Ideas to help:

➢ Re-organise your space so you can easily reach everything you need without clambering over things or moving everything to find what you need.

➢ Use cupboards, shelves and boxes, and labels with big writing so you can easily see what you need and where it is.

➢ Sort out your stationery drawer so you have easy access to pens, pencils, stapler, hole-punch, notebooks etc.

➢ Try to always put things back when you have finished with them. You'll find it much easier to find a pen or a file if it's in the right box.

➢ A quick vacuum and regular dusting will help keep things clean and tidy (plus, you never know what you'll find when you clean the top shelf or the back of the cupboard!).

Set daily, weekly, monthly, and longer goals

It might sound obvious, but typically you'll achieve more tasks and goals when you write them down.

This is because you're both physically and mentally committing to getting things done.

➢ Your brain is getting mentally engaged in thinking about the task.

➢ Your hand is physically writing the words and making your commitment visible in ink.

You might want to set daily, weekly, monthly, annual and longer goals. Once you've worked out what your goals are you can break them down into smaller steps.

Then using your time management skills you can allocate the time needed to make things happen.

Each person who reads this book will have different goals and different timeframes to achieve those goals.

Once your goals are written down they become achievable targets.

> ➤ Writing goals down gives you something visual to refer back to.

> ➤ There's a neurological connection between your hand writing the words and your brain receiving the instruction.

> ➤ You can assign time, people and/or resources to your goal.

> ➤ You can segment your goal into steps and tick each step as it gets done.

> ➤ Once achieved, you can look back at how you achieved your goals and set new ones.

Keep your goals where you can see them every day.

For example:

➢ Write your goals on sticky-notes and put them to your bathroom mirror or the fridge door.

➢ Create a screensaver with your goals written out so they're visible on your computer or laptop.

➢ Set up an alert on your phone to remind you of your goals at intervals throughout the week.

Make sure you can easily see what you're trying to achieve and it will become easier to do something towards your goals every day.

Remember - Every step towards your goal counts.

Remember - Celebrate each step!

What will you achieve in your time on Earth?

This might be a tough question, especially if it isn't something you've thought about before now.

Maybe you haven't had time to think about it. Maybe you haven't had a reason to think about it.

Sooner or later, most people want to know that what they've done with their lives has made a difference.

Maybe you know what you want to achieve in your time on this planet?

Maybe you've already achieved it?

Everyone has a talent and everyone can add value, no matter how big or how small you might think it is.

Call it leaving a legacy if you like.

If you're still thinking about this question, here are some ideas:

➢ Create something artistic

➢ Write a piece of music

➢ Invent a piece of technology

➢ Be part of a sports team

➢ Travel to a new country

➢ Learn a new language

Not everyone can or wants to leave a huge legacy. But being able to make a small difference in the world is something we can all achieve.

Jenny says: "I wanted to write stories for people to read and enjoy. I didn't want my time here to go without leaving something positive."

Be the difference to your neighbour, your family, your friends, colleagues and strangers.

Remember to write down what you want to achieve and it is more likely to happen.

Plan your short, medium, and long goals

Earlier we talked about setting short, medium and long term goals. After you have set your goals you'll need to make planning steps to make sure they happen.

For example:

> ➤ It might be difficult (if not impossible) to play football for your country if you haven't first played football in a local or regional team.

> ➤ But, before you joined a team, you would have attended training sessions, looked at fitness, changed your diet, made travel arrangements, organised childcare, the list goes on.

> ➤ Taking a step back again, you might have got the idea of playing football from watching the TV, or from playing football in the street or at school. You might have seen a friend playing football or been given a ball as a child.

If you reverse these steps, in a very simple ladder, they might look like this:

> ➢ I like the look of football on TV
> ➢ I want to play football with my friends
> ➢ I want to improve and be a better player
> ➢ I want to join a team
> ➢ I want to make football my career
> ➢ I want to play for my country

In this example, a short term goal would be to join a local football team and a long term goal would be to play football for your country.

It might be possible to achieve your short term goal in a few days, whereas the long term goal could take years.

Using a simple ladder of steps, you can write down what you want to achieve and then work backwards to fill in the gaps of how to achieve each goal step by step.

How much does your goal cost

Depending on what you wrote as your short term, medium and long term goals, you will probably have an idea of how much time, energy and money you'll need to invest to be able to achieve all or part of your goals.

You don't need everything in place to get started!

If your goal is to have a million pound turnover, it will start with one sale and build up from there.

If you want to have a million pound turnover this year, you'll need to know:

> ➢ How many days are left in the year?
> ➢ How much do you need to make each day?
> ➢ What if some days when you make nothing?

If your goal is to climb a mountain, what equipment will you need and how much will this cost?

Never let negative thoughts stop you achieving goals.

If you're thinking "I haven't got the money for doing this" then you're right.

If you change your thinking to "I'll start and see if the funds become available" you might find the right resources arrive at the right time.

Be aware of how much time, energy and money you need for each step of the way.

Review your goals regularly.

Reset and change direction where necessary.

Having some knowledge of the overall cost of your goal will help you stay on track and you don't need to have everything in place to get started.

Believe in your goals.

It's OK not to be busy all the time

It's OK to have quiet times. Sometimes rest and recovery is what you'll need to reset and recharge and you can carry on again.

It's important to listen to your body and your mind.

When you sense overwhelm, it is normally your body trying to tell you to take time out. It's saying you need to review what's going on and assess what is important.

If you leave your phone off-charge for long enough, the battery dies. The constant use drains the battery.

The same happens to your mind and your body. If you don't have down time, take a rest, or switch off, what happens?

Your body runs out of power and your recovery to full strength can be any length of time.

Everyone is different. You might feel refreshed after sitting for five minutes looking out of a window. Other people might be ready to go after a twenty minute power minute nap, a thirty minute meditation, or even a complete day off.

Rachael says: "I wasn't well recently, so I listened to my body and decided to have the day off. Dad came round to take Leo for a dog walk and asked, "What have you done today?". I said "nothing, I've put myself first and watched telly."

We're not suggesting you do this every day, but once in a while if your body seems to be telling you to take a rest, it isn't sensible to ignore it.

You'll be much more productive once you've had a rest, whether you are able to stop for five minutes, half an hour, or a full twenty-four hours.

It's OK not to be busy all the time!

Be aware of the time

You don't have to go far to see what time it is at any time of the day or night.

You might be wearing a watch with the time on your wrist, or you can check the clock on your phone, a wall clock, the cooker or TV.

There are plenty of time-telling devices outside too. You might be able to see a clock on a bus stop or train station, shop window, church tower, library, or in your car. In a park there might be sundials too!

You can use the time as an accurate measure to monitor where your time is being spent in relation to your goals.

One way to measure the time is to set an alarm on your phone. You can divide an hour into segments, e.g. 10, 15, 20 or 30 minutes, and try to achieve one of the steps towards your goal in that time.

Jenny says: "When doing chores, I put a time limit on each one and do my best to achieve the whole task in the timeframe. Some things take longer but having an 'end time' means I can do lots of different tasks without one thing taking over. I do the same for business tasks, never leaving something important half-done, but making sure I get around to doing lots of different tasks, all of which need attention."

Rachael says: "I schedule my week putting "Myself first" then time for "Family. Friends and Partner", then "Dog Walking time" followed by "Free Time". That's before looking at any work-related achievements for the week. By doing this and colour coding my spreadsheet, I can see at a glance how much time is being spent on each activity and also track anything I have procrastinated over or am finding overwhelming."

Plan your meals to save time deciding

Something that's helpful to plan ahead is food! Whether you think ahead to lunchtime or an evening meal for today, or plan a whole week ahead, is up to you.

Food is the fuel giving us the concentration and energy to achieve our tasks in the timeframe we want.

Most people work best when they're not hungry or thirsty (being dehydrated can reduce your performance too). You might find you're in a better mood, feel on top of things, make more calls or send more emails.

Rachael says: "I'm a real advocate of batch cooking. I use recipes that serve 4-6 people, so when cooking for myself and my husband, we get 3 meals from 1 cooking session. If I'm tired, I don't need to find the time to cook a meal from scratch."

Something that's helpful when planning meals to save time is writing a comprehensive shopping list. Instead of writing "Tuesday lasagne", write out each ingredient.

This helps when you're doing an online shop or at the supermarket, everything you need is written in black and white. It saves time thinking what you'll need.

Rachael says: "Mealtimes are important in our household and having a variety of healthy food available means there's always something nice to look forward to. When doing the batch cooking, I put portions into boxes, label them, and store them in the freezer."

What are your favourite meals?

Can you get larger recipes for these and do some batch cooking of your own?

The time you save can be put towards other tasks.

Wash, hang, put away

A laundry tip, but something that can be used in many different scenarios.

It's all about how doing things in sequence can help save time and enable you to use your time effectively.

Wash, hang, put away.

If you wash your clothes on Monday, hang them up to dry on Tuesday, and put them all away on Wednesday, it's taken you 3 goes to do 1 job!

If you don't put your washing away until Friday, then in essence it's taken 5 days to do 1 job (and maybe you'll have worn some of the clothes again before they even reached the wardrobe).

Depressing, isn't it!

However, if you are able to wash your clothes, hang them up to dry, and put them away on the same day, it'll take less brain power if you complete the task in a shorter timeframe.

Plus, it will free up your time for something else.

That's the aim of good time management – to free up your time for the things you love most.

Think about the sequences in your business. Is there anything you can change to streamline your processes?

For example, in a sales role, your sequence might be to phone Client A, take an order, invoice it, get paid, do the work, then phone Client B.

Each part of the customer order can be broken down into separate tasks, some of which you might choose to do sequentially, or some you could to do in batches.

If you can wash, hang and put away at the same time, you'll free up your time for something else.

Have you got the right lighting set up?

Don't underestimate the time saved by having the right environment to carry out your tasks.

If you're straining your eyes because you can't be bothered to turn the light on, it will be taking up extra brain power to read the words and extra time as your brain checks things before processing the information.

What if it took you 30 seconds to read this page in the optimum lighting and 2 minutes to read in a dim light.

That's 90 seconds more, just reading 1 page!

Scale it up and you can imagine how much extra time you would gain just from having the right lux level.

Having the correct lighting for your mobile phone, tablet, laptop or computer, makes all the difference too.

If the background light is too dim, it can strain your eyes and potentially cause long term damage. On the other hand, if the light is too bright and it might give you a headache.

If you're searching for something in your office, car or house, isn't it easier to use the lights or a torch rather than fumble around in the dark.?

Plus, it's probably safer too as you're less likely to bump into things.

Take a minute to check the lighting around you now.

Have you got the right lighting set up to maximise your performance on your current task?

The right lighting is good for your eyes and can save time you'll be able to use elsewhere.

Watch a candle

It's important to give you brain some downtime, to allow it to decompress and to process all the thoughts that it's been processing during the day.

Rachael says: "I enjoy lighting a candle at the end of the working day (before seeing family or friends). I concentrate on the flickering flame for 5 to 10 minutes and it gives me time to process things that have happened during the day."

By focussing on the flame you allow your subconscious to process all the thoughts, tasks, challenges and wins you've dealt with during the day.

By giving your brain this brief "time out" period you're allowing yourself to change your focus of thoughts from work to family.

It's a break between activities.

Taking these moments to decompress your thoughts whilst watching the candle gently flickering takes your attention back to yourself.

It gives you the opportunity to put aside thinking about tasks, emails, conversations, processes, and enables you to switch across to living in the moment with your family and loved ones.

If you haven't got a candle or somewhere safe to light one, there are plenty of places where you can watch candles online and you'll have the similar experience.

Rachael says: "Get a wax melt or a fake flickering flame. It's not quite as good as a real candle, but it's better than nothing!"

Try it!

Allocate some downtime to recalibrate

A key part of your time management is to include regular downtime where you have time and space to recharge and recalibrate your thoughts.

> ➤ Time
> ➤ Space
> ➤ Recharge

Your downtime might look different compared with other people, but what works for them might not work for you, and vice versa.

For example, your downtime might be a relaxing bath, reading a book, taking the dog for a walk or playing a game of tennis. It might be indoors or outdoors. It might be sporty or sedentary.

What matters is the allocation of regular downtime in between your tasks.

It might feel like a waste of your time to be doing nothing for an hour or two, but it gives your mind the freedom to process, catch-up, and begin again.

If it helps, think of your downtime in the same way as filling up your car with fuel, or putting your phone on charge. You wouldn't get far without it!

Downtime ensures you have the energy to do your next project to the best of your ability.

Always allow a time buffer

One of the top tips we can offer is to allow a few extra minutes around each of your tasks.

With the best will in the world very few days, if any days, go to the perfect plan.

> ➢ Your best friend might call with an emergency.
> ➢ A delivery might arrive ahead of schedule.
> ➢ The dog walk might take longer than planned.
> ➢ Or, you might just not feel like doing it today.

Things can, and will, crop up!

If you have unexpected interruptions in your day they can take you over 20 minutes to get back to the level of concentration you were at before they happened.

So, it makes sense to plan free time within your day.

These time buffers mean you have already made a section of time available where you can move a task into that timeslot, should a disruption occur.

If you don't include time buffers in your daily plan, you might find it stressful transitioning between tasks.

You might have to push another task to the next day which causes tomorrow's plan to be disrupted before it even starts!

Give yourself time.

Include time buffers between your tasks and review your schedule of tasks regularly to check if there are any areas where it would be helpful to extend (or reduce) the buffer and make the best use of your time.

Time out for YOU is a good thing

The most important person in your life is YOU!

Without you, you can't be employed, you won't have family or friends, you wouldn't have a business and you wouldn't have life!

When you are on a plane, you are told to put your own oxygen mask on first. It's so you're ok before you start helping others.

For exactly the same reason, the most important person in your life, is the same for everyone.

YES that's correct!

The most important person in your life is the same as everyone else!

IT'S YOU

Or to put it another way, "It's ME, MYSELF and I".

When thinking about time management, it's important to take care of yourself.

Rachael says: "If you switch to referring to having 'myself time' rather than 'me time' it resonates with our brains and allows us to look after myself as well as helping others. We often say 'look after yourself' to other people, so why not say 'look after myself' to yourself?"

If you think putting "me" first seems selfish, remember until you put yourself first you can't help anyone else.

This means putting your mindset, your nutrition and your happiness at the forefront of your planning, before you look into business related tasks.

So, take a little time out for YOU.

If you don't like reading try listening

If you struggle to find the time to read, then consider investing in audio books. There are millions to choose from, so you're sure to find something you'll enjoy.

You can listen to an audio book while you're walking, driving, hanging up or putting away the washing, making tea, in between meetings, at almost any time of the day or night.

It's a great way of using your time twice – you can be doing something and listening at the same time.

Rachael says: "A friend of mine recently had open heart surgery and they were feeling quite low whilst in recovery (at the hospital and at home afterwards) with little energy, even to hold a book. So, instead of sending them a paperback, I gave them an ebook, which they loved!"

Remember why you want to manage your time

Why do you want to get back control of your time?

Do you want to manage your time better so you can make more money? If yes, why?

Do you want to manage your time better so you can spend more time with your family? If yes, what will you do together?

Do you want to go on holiday? If yes, when and where?

Put a date in your diary now for when you want this to happen. Speak to a travel agent or search for holidays online.

Writing it down makes it more likely to happen.

Something to remember when dividing up your time between family, friends and work is that it's not just the time you're spending, but also the buffer of time around the event.

For example, if you're going on holiday you might want to build time into your plan for the flight time, the time to recover from jetlag, the time to catch up on all the things that have come in whilst you were away.

You may wish to add an extra day to your "return to work" date as a buffer where you can use the time to catch up on admin before your clients expect responses.

Another option is to scale your "return to work" date so that not all of your clients think you're back on the same day. This will help make things more manageable.

If you spend time planning for these extra factors it will give you more time to enjoy while you're away.

Remember to set your "out of office" messages so your customers know you'll be back soon.

Watch a training video while cooking tea

Watching a training video while doing something else is a great way to use your time twice. It doesn't have to be done while cooking tea, you could be doing the ironing or working out in your home gym.

Rachael says: "I enjoy learning new things and upgrading my skills through watching training videos. If you have a Smart TV you can watch videos online and benefit from a louder volume than your laptop or computer. This makes it easier to hear over your cooking."

Training videos can be training on anything from a skill you'd like to learn, self-development, a process which you're not confident with, or a hobby that interests you.

What training videos would you like to watch? Is there something new you would love to learn?

Where does your time go?

Are there times when you feel like you have been really productive, but at the same time feel as though you've achieved nothing?

Have you ever wondered where your time goes?

If this is you, write a list of five things you did this morning from memory:

1. _____

2. _____

3. _____

4. _____

5. _____

Now write down how long each thing took.

Is it as much time as you expected? Did something take more time than it needed to take?

If you want to make further investigations into where you're spending your time, you can use a Time Tracker.

A Time Tracker can be as simple as a sheet of paper or spreadsheet where you record the time and task.

Using a Time Tracker over the course of a week or a month will enable you to see patterns.

With the extra information, you'll be able to spot areas you might want to change.

The Time Tracker will help you identify tasks you can outsource, delegate, or stop doing altogether.

Jenny says: "Sometimes, I'll finish the day with things I want to do but have run out of time, energy, or both. Just having a quick mental or written recall of the day reminds me it hasn't been a waste of time and I've achieved more than I thought!"

Use tech to prompt the start and end of a task

It can be easy to lose track of time.

If you have lots to do each task can run into the next task. Or maybe, if you don't have much to do, your time can quickly evaporate and you'll be wondering where the day has gone.

Using a little bit of technology can be a big help.

If you've got loads and loads of tasks to do in a day or a week it can be overwhelming and stressful.

With time management, you're compartmentalising the tasks into manageable segments. You're working out which are your productive hours for each type of task.

Something extra you might find helpful is to set an alarm to prompt you at different times of the day.

The alarm can be audible, a bell, or chime, programmed to sound at a set time. Or your alarm could be a light coming on, or going off, or a flashing light to get your attention.

Whichever works best for you.

The alarm is designed to prompt you:

> ➢ To alert you to an absolute change of task, e.g. switching from doing the invoicing to collecting children from school.

> ➢ Or the alarm can be a countdown timer, e.g. your alarm could be set to go off 15 minutes before you need to move on to the next task.

Using alerts and alarms can be helpful to manage your time without needing to watch the clock.

Your digital assistant is counting all the minutes for you and gently nudging you when it's time to move on.

Use an online calendar for calls and events

Using an online calendar has several benefits and gives the opportunity to share appointments with family and colleagues.

Rachael says: "I share a calendar with my husband and we use it to add lots of different events. One example is each week I add the time for our supermarket Click and Collect and also the time buffer for the driving time there and back. The great thing about this is that I don't need to remember to say that we need to go and pick up the shopping. He likes it because he doesn't need to ask me what time we need to be there!"

Once the appointments are added into the calendar each person receives a notification. This saves lots of time and avoids any miscommunications.

Put work and available times in your calendar

On the theme of shared calendars, do you use a visible work calendar your clients and potential clients can view to see when you're available, and when you're not?

Or, do you play phone ping pong when you're trying to set up meetings?

> ➤ You try calling someone and leave a voicemail.
> ➤ They call you back but you can't take the call so they leave a message on your voicemail.
> ➤ You try calling again and get their voicemail so you change to a text message or even email.

This going backwards and forwards is both frustrating and time consuming. Although each occurrence doesn't take up a lot of time, collectively the time playing ping pong with messages all adds up. It's time that could be saved and used on something you enjoy more!

If you use an online calendar, you can control who can see different parts of your week.

You can allocate time on different days that's visible to your existing clients, or to new customers, for training sessions, and time reserved for family and friends.

You can also control which time slots are offered to people in your different categories. For example, you can make the time between 6pm and 8pm visible to friends, and the time between 10am and 5pm visible to clients and prospective clients.

There are web-based systems (free and paid versions) which link to your existing online calendar and check to see when you are free before offering slots to people.

You can personalise both your online calendar and the appointment booking system with your own words, colours and branding to the extent people feel they are booking the appointment directly with you.

Life is like a computer program

Once you're on a roll with managing your time you'll find that some tasks are almost autonomous, a bit like a computer program running a loop.

You'll program your brain to be doing something while something else is going on, ending the task when it is finished and starting the next task.

For example, a "Do While, End If" loop might include doing social media posts while children are at school and ending the task when it's time to collect them.

Another example could be to make sales calls while you're printing company brochures, ending the loop when either all the sales calls are made, or when the printer has stopped printing.

In Time Management, you're **using your time twice** doing something while something else is going on too.

Make it simple to access your contacts

How easy is it for you to find Customer X's contact details? What about the phone number for the electric company, car garage, or your next door neighbour?

You'll save lots of time (and stress) if you have easy access to your phone book and email addresses.

Make it simple to store and retrieve contact details.

Using a single online database for your contacts gives you one place to look. It means you can store more than just a name and a number.

If you make sales calls and catch-up calls, how easy is it for you to access Mr and Mrs Smith's number? Or their email address? Do you know when you last spoke with them? Or what they last ordered?

Create one place to look with everything you need.

Make it simple to reach your contact's phone and email details and you'll save a fair amount of time compared with scrabbling around for business cards or loading up a web browser to do an online search.

Rachael says: "I recommend using a single database (stored in the cloud if practical) where you can list and categorise your contacts and have one-click access to phone or email them 24x7."

If you can make it easy to find your contacts you'll save plenty of time over the course of a year.

It might be a minute here or ten minutes there, but overall, you'll be reclaiming lost time and also managing your time more effectively.

Time management is not just about managing the activities you do with your time, it's about checking your systems and processes to make sure you're making the best use of the time you have available.

Aeroplane Mode

Remember, each and every time you get distracted it takes around 20 minutes to get back to the same level of concentration before you were distracted.

It doesn't take much to get distracted.

> ➤ The flash of light from your social media.
> ➤ The ping of an incoming text message.
> ➤ The pop-up scroll bar with information.
> ➤ A number in a red circle next to the app.
> ➤ The ring of your phone when someone calls.
> ➤ The zzzzz if your phone is set to vibrate.

Technology infiltrates many of our senses and you may feel as though you have been programmed to expect an interruption at certain times of the day.

It's also possible you're receiving a notification from someone else's scheduled call, post or email, and not from something that needs your attention right now!

You can put your phone "on silent", but it will still ring and the caller may think you're ignoring them (and they might be right).

But, if you turn on the Aeroplane Mode your phone will divert to voicemail and notifications will be muted.

It tells people that your out of reach (or out of range) for now. This can give a more favourable impression, that you're busy or unavailable, rather than ignoring them or slow to answer.

When a call goes straight through to voicemail, the caller may think "they're on the phone, they'll call me back when they're free, that's ok" and they are more receptive to your call when you do call them back.

Aeroplane Mode also stops you receiving notifications from platforms too, so once you've achieved the task you're working on, you can see everything and respond without interrupting your concentration.

You can use Aeroplane Mode without being in a plane!

Delete old data

Hands up if you enjoy having a good clear out and decluttering of your home, garage, car, or office!

Typically we're pretty good at occasionally, or maybe more frequently, clearing out our food cupboards, our clothes or sorting through trinkets.

> ➢ It creates space for new things.
> ➢ It makes it easier to find old things.

However, when was the last time you reviewed all the documents you have on your laptop, your mobile phone, or files stored in the cloud?

It makes sense that the more data you keep, the more complicated the filing system and the harder it is to find something.

There comes a point where it becomes frustrating with the wasted time looking for things.

The frustration can lead to becoming irritable and rows with family, friends, colleagues and maybe clients. That's not good!

As part of your time management, always allow extra time for virtual housekeeping. Tidy up your computer desktop. File documents and images in sensible places.

With the promise of unlimited storage it hasn't been necessary to delete old data. We've become an age of data hoarders (and in many professions we need to retain years of data).

Ask yourself these questions:

1.   Why did I write this or photograph this?
2.   When did I last look at this?
3.   Is it still relevant to hold onto?
4.   What benefit do I get from keeping it?

If you sort your files from the oldest to the newest you'll be able to see potentially years of your digital footprint. A whole lifetime of data.

It can be overwhelming and that's a reason why many people choose not to start. It's easy to keep everything.

But if keeping everything in a higgledy-piggledy, jumble of files is taking your brain power away from other tasks, it's time for a sort out!

Set aside 15 minutes (and add it to your calendar) to start your data decluttering.

Rachael says: "When you start deleting old data you might find it so cathartic you end up spending an hour or so doing it."

Decluttering can also apply to social media contacts or names stored in your phone or email contacts.

- ➢ Do I know this person?
- ➢ Am I interested in their news?
- ➢ What benefit is it to stay connected?

Your answer determines whether they stay or go!

Pin tabs

Pinning tabs is a great way to have multiple tabs appear in the same order when you open your browser.

Another bonus feature from pinning your tabs is that it's harder for notifications to attract your attention.

The reason for this is because each tab is much smaller, often just the logo, so you are not as easily distracted by messages and notifications arriving, especially if you mute the tabs as well.

To pin a tab in most browsers, right click on the tab and choose "pin". Easy!

"When Rachael told me about the ability to pin tabs it was a game changer! No longer was I spending time scrolling through multiple tabs to find my calendar, my chats or messenger, they were always the first 3 tabs whenever I opened my browser."

It's simple, effective and saves time!

Mute tabs

Muting tabs is a brilliant way to make sure you are only focussed on the tab window you are working on.

It stops your concentration being broken by a "ping" and then looking to see which platform made the noise.

By muting a tab you have control over how and when you respond to tags and messages, not the browser controlling your time.

To mute a tab, in most browsers, right click on the tab and chose "mute".

"The amount of time I saved by muting individual tabs was astounding. I had never realised you could mute individual tabs until Rachael told me and now I only look at notifications when I want to, I don't get distracted from a task by that "ping" and I can get so much more done with my time."

Muting tabs helps you concentrate on your tasks.

Background noise, yes or no?

This tip is open for discussion as you might change your mind whether you want background noise in different situations.

Are you the sort of person who likes the radio on?

Does having a constant channel of chatter and tunes help you produce your best results?

Do you find there's a difference between listening to your favourite CD (where you know all the words and the beats) compared with random music, adverts and chat, on the radio?

Or do you work best in silence?

The same goes for the TV, although are you tempted to look up frequently to see what's happening?

Looking up is great if it's a screen break from your computer or tablet.

Not so great if the TV is a distraction and you lose momentum getting back into whatever you were doing.

When thinking about your preference for background noise, remember the noise can include your family or work colleagues going about their own tasks in the same room.

Is someone clumping up and down the stairs? Are they opening and closing doors?

Maybe there's a dog barking, birds singing, or a cat fight somewhere outside. You might tune into traffic noise from cars, planes or trains.

Does it help or hinder your progress?

Equally, long periods of silence might not be your cup of tea either. There might be times when having absolute silence helps you concentrate on a tricky task.

You might prefer silence if you need to make an important phone call or write an important email.

When you know how much background noise you can tolerate and still get quality results from your tasks, make a note, and see if you can recreate your optimum working conditions on a regular basis.

You might see the need to change your work pattern to a different time of day, or a different day of the week, to get the best results.

Lots of the noise could happen outside of your control, but you can optimise your day to work at your best during the times when you have control of the noise levels around you.

You also have the option to wear some noise-cancelling earplugs or headphones playing your favourite music.

Have a think about the type of music you're playing too. Something loud and fast might help get boring jobs done. Rainforest or ocean sounds can be calming.

Tidy working space

One of the biggest "time thieves" can be trying to work in a messy environment. It's those minutes we waste looking for things that could be put to better use.

For example, you have an online board meeting coming up at 11 o'clock today. You want your clean green shirt to wear. Where is it? What's the online meeting code? What about a pen and notebook? How about tidying up a bit so your background doesn't look messy?

Lots of questions and perhaps at least one of these sounds familiar! It can be exhausting and easily solved with a little preparation.

Being able to find things quickly saves a lot of time and stress. Making time to create a tidy working (and living) space is guaranteed to save you so much time over the course of your lifetime.

Not just today, or this week, but your whole life!

Supposing you spent 5 minutes looking for your car keys this morning, scale it up and that's around an hour of time over the course of a month!

What else could you do with that time?

A tidy working space is arguably better for your health (less stressful, more hygienic) as well as for people around you. It's possible your messy desk or office might make other people feel stressed or distressed.

It doesn't have to take much effort to create a tidy working space.

If you save a little time at the end of your task before starting the next task you'll soon form a habit that enables you to put away what you've been using.

This frees up the space for next time or for the next person to use the space. Plus it gives you a blank canvas for being creative without being weighed down by whatever you were doing earlier.

Take the kitchen as an example. Doesn't it feel better to walk into a clean kitchen with lots of possibilities?

Whether you're making a cup of tea or preparing dinner, if you can get straight to what you need rather than wading through dirty dishes, you can guarantee you'll feel better and it will take less time.

"Everything in its place and a place for everything."

Make time to find a place for everything you have in your office. Those lever arch files or that mountain of business cards. That cup from this morning. Where do they need to go? Everything in its place is a great time management tip that's easy to introduce.

Invest in a new bookcase if it helps. Have a sort out of your desk drawers. You'll find space for everything and if there isn't space for something, do you really need it?

Having a tidy space saves time, energy and possibly money if you find something buried in clutter you thought you'd lost or need to replace too.

Touch once emails

Be honest. How many times do you look at an email before you do something with it?

> ➢ Once
> ➢ More than once

If it's only once then you're already doing this tip. If you look at an email more than once, why?

The "Touch Once" method is a great way to streamline how long it takes you to reply to incoming emails.

When managing your time it can be helpful to set aside dedicated time slots in your day to check your emails.

To avoid interruptions and ad-hoc notifications, you can set your device to download emails at set intervals.

Then you can apply the "Touch Once" principle.

You literally just touch the email once.

Using the details included with the email (the sender, the subject, the preview text), you can make choices.

- ➢ You can choose whether to delete it.
- ➢ You can choose whether to file it.
- ➢ You can choose whether to reply to it.

If you only looked at each email once, how much time would you save?

How many megabytes of storage space could you clear and how much brain power would you free up?

It all helps because your subconscious isn't thinking about multiple possibilities.

You're not weighed down thinking about a payment you need to make or where you filed a Zoom link because using the "Touch Once" method you know you've already transferred all the details you need from the email into your calendar.

Use time blocks to do just one task at a time

Time blocks are a great way to separate your day into manageable segments.

Think of them like building blocks where you can stack one block on top of another. The blocks don't need to be the same size, but they must all fit together.

Creating the time blocks is a way to divide up your time to match the tasks you want to achieve. Each time block will contain a task, or part of a task.

Your time blocks can be an hour of time divided into 15 minute segments, or you can divide a day, week, or month into flexible time blocks which fit around your other commitments.

Time blocks are building blocks which fit together.

An example of using time blocks is to apply this method to an event with a start and finish time, such as football practice, which might take place from 7pm to 8.30pm every Wednesday.

In your calendar, you would have a time block starting at 6.30pm to allow time for travelling to the football practice and getting changed into your football kit. The travelling time block might be variable in size if you offer to pick up a friend to take to training on alternate Wednesdays.

The football training activity would have it's own time block because it has a fixed start and finish time. Then the third time block is used for your homeward travel. This can be variable in size too, for example if you stop to get a takeaway on your way back one week.

Earlier in your calendar, there might be a time block for having tea at home. You could put this in for 6pm to allow enough time to eat before travelling and getting changed.

Before tea, your time block might be a client meeting at 5pm to 5.30pm, with a 30 minute commute before you get home at 6pm for tea.

You can see how time blocks fill your calendar with extra details surrounding the activities you carry out.

In another example, if you have a free morning on Tuesdays, you could divide the time from 9am to midday into 15 minute time blocks and see what you can achieve in each time block.

Write down what you did in those 15 minute time blocks. Use the information to make any changes.

Was there anywhere you felt was wasted time?

By separating your time into time blocks for achieving a specific task the idea is that you don't start anything else (unless it's really urgent) in that time block.

It gives you the freedom to focus fully on the task you're trying to complete.

Don't worry if you don't finish what you started in the time block as there will be times when a time block will overrun, or may not even start if you haven't received all the details to complete a task.

For example if you were put on hold for ten minutes in a phone conversation and wanted to wait for the caller to return, you can extend your time block or push the next time block and next task further into your day.

Remember, anything that isn't time-sensitive (like the example with the fixed football training schedule) can be rescheduled into a new time block, either tomorrow, or for a later date.

Rachael says: "I use time blocks to separate activities in my day. Each time block has a start time and a finish time and I can easily see what needs to be done in each segment. The time blocks can be moved around if needed too."

Set up and use a Time Intensity Grid

If you haven't heard of a Time Intensity Grid before, it's an easy to use square to help with prioritising tasks.

Your square is divided into quarters and you drop tasks into each quarter. This categorises the task by how much time it will take and how much energy it needs.

How do you currently prioritise tasks?

Do you write them one underneath each other in a sequential list? Or a random list as and when things occur to you?

Maybe you assign numbers to the items on your list.

- The order you thought of them.
- The importance of the task.
- The ones which will bring in the most money.
- The tasks you enjoy the most (or the least).

Your list might subconsciously be ordered in the sequence of the tasks you are best at the top and the ones you feel you're worst at are at the end of your list.

If you are focussing your tasks in this way you are not taking account of how much energy a task takes.

> Rachael says: "In my coaching sessions, I encourage clients to create Time Intensity Grids. It offers an insight into the tasks which need to be done and helps prioritise their workload."

The Time Intensity Grid works by categorising tasks in terms of intensity and time.

The word "Intensity" is chosen on purpose because it can mean something different to everyone. A task you find easy might be extremely difficult for someone else.

"After my power hour with Rachael, I now know what I need to do, when I need to do it and what brings me in the most money."

Intensity could be interpreted as:

➢ The energy the task drains from you

➢ The confidence you have in doing a task

➢ What it stops you from doing (do you need to be 100% focussed on just that thing?)

➢ Could you be using that time twice?

➢ Your skillset and knowledge of the task

➢ Your self–belief in the task or project

➢ Your passion for the task

Jenny says: "I write grids on paper to see what needs to be done and by when. It helps me categorise what's important and what's likely to take a lot of time, or energy. Then I can assign each task into the grid and give it my best working time."

Here is Rachael's Time Intensity Grid. Make a copy and start filling out the tasks versus the time they will take and the intensity they require from you.

High Intensity / High Time	High Intensity / Low Time
Low Intensity / High Time	Low Intensity / Low Time

Use numbered lists to set the order of tasks

Hopefully through reading the tips in this book you're on board with the idea of creating a list of things you want to achieve on a daily basis.

You can call it a "To Do List" if you like or maybe you prefer to refer to it as an "Achievement List".

Rachael says: "I prefer 'Achievement List' because as you tick things off they are your achievements and it feels good to achieve things doesn't it!"

So, you've got a list.

It could be a shopping list. It could be a list of clients you want to call to find out if they want more of your products or services.

Your list might be a mixture of home and work tasks (some people prefer to separate the lists, or have a combined list, it's whatever works best for you).

For example, feeding the dog might be your first task on Monday and taking your car to the garage might be your number one task on Tuesday. Which task you put first can vary day by day or month by month.

You can adjust the priority if something crops up.

On the whole, you would assign number one to the first task you want to achieve, then two, then three, and continue until each task has a priority.

It's important to do this quickly, otherwise assigning numbers to tasks can become a task in itself!

Start with number one and carry on until everything is either done or if it needs to be moved to tomorrow, or sometime in the future, it will appear on your future task list and you don't need to worry about it today!

Plan tomorrow's tasks today

By spending time at the end of each day reviewing the things you have achieved (and sometimes things you were hoping to do, but didn't) you will be preparing yourself to get a head start in the morning.

If there's something you wanted to do but didn't achieve it, then this is a great opportunity to reflect and review.

Is it OK to move that task to tomorrow?

What happened?

- Was it a "low importance task" and therefore wasn't a priority?
- Is the task overwhelming and you need to break it down into smaller chunks?
- Was it just that something unexpected came up and got in your way?

Taking the time to reflecting and review may give you an insight into what's happened in the day.

Do you need to plan more free time and time buffers into your day so you have space to move things to when something more important comes up?

At the end of today review things:

> What you have achieved
> What you didn't achieve

Spend a little time examining why you did or didn't achieve them.

Are these tasks a high enough priority to move to tomorrow, or can they be put on the backburner to be done at some future point?

Everyday our prioritise and life changes, it's OK to be flexible with your plans too.

Use colours to prioritise tasks

Colours make things brighter and bright colours make things stand out!

Using lots of different colours in can help differentiate between people, tasks, days of the week, priorities and much more.

Why not let technology do the hard work for you?

If you use a spreadsheet it's easy to add conditional formatting to cells.

An example of this is to change the background colour of a cell, or the font colour, size or style, based on criteria in rules you set up.

Great uses of conditional formatting are to show which tasks are due to be done today, or tomorrow, or to highlight tasks which should have already been done.

You can also use conditional formatting to order your tasks by when you want to complete them.

For example if you have a task which needs to be carried out by midday, then your spreadsheet can be set up so that it automatically changes the colour of any incomplete morning tasks from yellow to red.

Bright colours will draw your attention to areas you need to check. This can save lots of time scrolling up and down inside your spreadsheet searching for what needs to be done.

Using different colours may help you see which tasks you are procrastinating over. It will highlight the tasks which you never seem to get round to completing.

With the extra information, you can ask yourself why the tasks are taking so much time, or maybe there's something external that's holding up the task.

Use colours to help manage your time.

Don't let housework take over your life

Remember we're talking about managing your time at home as well as your time at work. It's all part of the same 24 hours in the day.

There's a "Two Minute Rule" which is a great way to manage your time on "important but not urgent" tasks.

If you see something that can be done in two minutes or less, the advice is to do it now, while you're on your way to another task.

What can be done at home in two minutes?

> ➤ Taking the rubbish bins out
> ➤ Clearing up breadcrumbs on the table
> ➤ Putting away clothes from the dryer
> ➤ Checking for upcoming appointments
> ➤ Writing a list of what you want to achieve next

What can be done at work in two minutes?

> Filing paperwork

> Hoovering the reception area

> Phoning home to check in with your family

> Writing a list of what you want to achieve next

Those two minutes here and there throughout the day can be filled with things to contribute to your overall time management goals.

Don't do tomorrow what you can do today.

Taking two minutes to sort something, tidy something, call someone, whatever you choose, will add up to lots of little things being done at home and in your office.

You'll be surprised what you can fit into two minutes when you're really focussed on getting something done.

You can always set an alert, countdown timer, or an alarm on your phone to signal when the two minutes is up and it's time to move on to the next activity.

Create an Achievement List (not a To Do List)

A quick Yes / No question to start this tip. There's no problem if you do or you don't, but it may help with various areas at home and at work if you do.

The question is:

Do you use lists?

> *Rachael says: "This is the question I ask all my new clients and it's very interesting the responses I get!"*

Generally speaking, most people write a list at least once in a while. It might be a list of clients to call, or the people invited to a house party. A pretty common list would be a shopping list (whether you remember to take it with you to the supermarket is another matter!).

There is a large difference between calling your list a "TO DO" list and calling it an "Achievement List".

The reason for this is simply because if you refer to it as a "TO DO List", your eyes and your subconscious focuses on everything you haven't achieved.

In your mind, the items "TO DO" are a mountain to climb and you may start the day with a feeling of overwhelm and despair.

"Crumbs! There's so much on this list, I'm only going to add to it and I'm never going to get everything done!"

However, if you reframe your list and change its name to an "Achievement List" your eyes and subconscious focuses on what you have achieved.

*"Wow, what a lot I've achieved today.
What more can I achieve?"*

Also, leave your achievements on the list (crossed out or with ticks) so you remember you've done well today!

Check emails at set times

If you can set aside focussed time to check your emails this will means you're in control of when you let other people's messages influence your day.

Rachael says: "Through networking, I've met people who set their email program to only check for new emails at specific times of the day. The system might be set up to check first thing in the morning, at lunchtime and mid-afternoon. Or a popular setting was for every fifteen minutes."

It's important to decide for yourself how frequently you want to check for new emails. Your work might dictate that receiving emails day and night is the best system.

You can configure your phone, tablet, or computer to check for new emails all the time, or at set times, or wait for you to press "send and receive". It's up to you.

We decide for ourselves when we will check and action our emails. We decide at what point in the day we'll look at the messages, questions, problems and sales pitches other people would like us to deal with.

One thing you may wish to consider is not checking your emails first thing. Allow yourself time to settle into the day and then open the floodgates.

Depending on the type of emails you receive will dictate how long it will take you to investigate, reply and resolve any issues.

Although you may have set aside thirty minutes for checking your email, it's possible one of the emails, or the actions you need to take, are more complex than can be achieved in the timeslot.

Dealing with time consuming and unscheduled requests can capsize your plans for the day. Are you ready for other people's demands before opening your email!

Start your day in a positive way.

Check social media at set times

Whilst it's very tempting to check social media as soon as you see that blue light, hear that ping or see that pop up notification, don't do it!

➢ What's that?

➢ I don't want to miss out!

➢ It'll just take a second...

That quick check you promised yourself can quickly turn into a quarter of an hour, or more!

The reality of the situation is, will anyone die if you don't read that notification? Probably not! Will you starve if you don't read that notification? Probably not! Will you lose your house if you don't read that notification? Probably not!

The most important thing to remember with effective time management is that **you control your time**.

With this in mind, the best way to keep control of your time is to check your social media when you want to.

If it helps, log out of Facebook, Tick Tock, Instagram, LinkedIn, WhatsApp, Pintrest, (and any other social media) and only open each one when you have the time available to look at (and act on) the notifications.

If your work relies on using communication apps such as WhatsApp or Messenger, have a look at one of the systems which enable you to see your messages across multiple platforms, but doesn't show you individual post notifications.

> *Rachael says: "This saves me so much time! I turn on the 'Focus' mode which turns off all notifications for as long as I want without needing to log out of any of the social platforms."*

Try it! How much time would you save simply by not being distracted by social media notifications?

Outsource graphics if you don't think in pictures

When creating your marketing or social media posts using pictures is a great way of attracting attention.

However, what do you do if you don't think in pictures? Maybe you don't see yourself as creative or are worried about how and where to start.

Rachael says: "I much prefer working with spreadsheets than images. For me, it takes so much time thinking about which picture to use, that I find it easier to delegate this to someone else!"

If this is you, and you need to create eye-catching graphics and info-graphics, find someone you trust to do it for you.

Outsourcing is a key part of time management.

The amount of stress, overwhelm, time and energy you could be spending trying to find the perfect match, could far outweigh the cost of delegating the task.

> ➤ It should be possible to make your money back and much more from delegating searching for images and creating eye-catching graphics.

> ➤ You'll have more time available to spend with your family and friends, and on other activities you'd rather be doing.

The reward from outsourcing a stressful task is likely to be far-reaching and produce results you never imagined.

If you're not convinced, try it on a low-risk basis.

Test this theory by making a small investment in one or two graphics from a professional designer.

You can check the results from your marketing and also make sure you have done something you wanted to do with the extra time you have saved.

Give yourself time without distractions

These are great reasons why it's important to stick to doing one task with zero interruptions:

- ➢ It gets done faster.
- ➢ It gets done more accurately.
- ➢ It gets done with less stress.

With practice, you can tune out things that might distract you:

- ➢ Road traffic noise.
- ➢ Noise from planes or trains.
- ➢ People talking down the corridor.
- ➢ Birdsong or dogs barking.
- ➢ General noise from the floors above or below if you work in a multi-level building.
- ➢ A phone ringing.

Almost anything can distract you!

Distractions affect our senses in different ways.

You might find you get distracted by the light levels in your working environment. A flickering bulb, the light too bright (or dim), affects your performance.

The smell of freshly brewed coffee from the cafe next door might be a distraction.

Sudden noises, such as a driver beeping their car horn or a dog bark could affect your concentration. Equally the continuous noise of a lawnmower, chainsaw, or building works can take its toll.

Maybe you're distracted because you're hungry or thirsty. Even being too hot or too cold can affect your productivity and time management.

If you can reduce or eliminate distractions, you'll find you can focus for longer, and achieve more on your list of tasks each day.

How you handle distractions is the difference.

Find a way to see things differently

Squirrels* are fun to watch aren't they!

But, however much squirrels are really interesting and relaxing to watch as they go about their business, they don't add anything to your time.

When thinking about time management, it's easy to focus only on the main things you're procrastinating over or feel overwhelmed by.

Rachael says: "What mindset do you need to change in order to realise how much control over your time you do have?

* *Squirrels are Rachael's favourite way to describe how something can pop up and distract us from what we're supposed to be doing!*

Accept that things won't be perfect

It would be easy if life ran smoothly, wouldn't it!

We all know things can (and will) crop up from time to time that throw everything out of kilter.

It's how you react that counts.

> ➤ It's easy to get angry.
> ➤ Easy to blame others.
> ➤ Easy to write the day off.

It's much harder to take that deep breath.

> ➤ To accept things haven't gone as you hoped.
> ➤ Things aren't always as you expected.

A tactic is to **ringfence** the situation, to draw a virtual boundary around the person, incident, or whatever hasn't gone to plan.

You might consider calling it damage limitation.

➢ What is affected by what's happened?

➢ What is outside of your control?

If you can create a mental barrier between yourself and the situation it can make it less stressful.

Another tactic is to **reframe** the situation, to see things from a different perspective. Consider it an alternative version of events, creating a positive spin if you can.

➢ Can you see any possibilities in the situation?

➢ Is there anyone you know who can help?

➢ Can you help someone in the same situation?

If you can, (and it won't always be possible) force yourself to smile when something disrupts your day. It's important to **carry on**, one step at a time, towards your goal and destination.

Ringfence. Reframe. Carry On.

It's OK to get distracted sometimes

If you've lost time today through one or more distractions getting in the way of what you've been trying to achieve, it's OK.

> ➤ Be kind to yourself.
> ➤ You've clocked that it's a distraction.

Maybe the distraction is a sign for you to check where you're spending your time.

It's a chance to stop and review your daily plan.

It can take up to 20 minutes to get back in the zone for carrying on with your task.

It can take even longer than 20 minutes if you keep getting distracted.

Stop and check.

Thinking back to earlier tasks, has something in your immediate environment distracted you?

> ➤ What has distracted you?
> ➤ Why has it distracted you?
> ➤ How can you react?
> ➤ Do you need to do something about it?

Can you change the noise level by working from home, a café, or your car?

Remember, it's ok to get distracted (we all get distracted from time to time). It's part of life and it's normal.

It's how you deal the distraction that counts.

Remove things that aren't helping

This tip is to encourage you to remove anything that isn't actively contributing towards your current task or a step towards your overall goal.

Take a moment to look around you.

When did you last have a declutter of your desk, your office, review your day, or drop things that are no longer important?

> Rachael says: "A proper declutter of your desktop and office can make space for new ideas. It's not just a quick tidy-up, a proper declutter gets you to remove everything that isn't making a positive difference."

A proper declutter of your laptop, tablet, phone or computer can make it run faster and give easy access to the files you need.

A proper declutter of your car can reveal a lot about your lifestyle. Is there any reason why you didn't pop your on-the-go sandwich wrapper and fizzy drink can into a rubbish bin, when you probably pass several bins on your route from home to work and back again?

Remove it! Declutter it!

Getting bogged down with virtual or physical clutter can seriously hamper your time management and your ability to smash your goals.

So, remove ANYTHING and EVERYTHING that's holding you back. Sometimes you can get a feel for whether it's something you need to keep, bin, recycle or give away.

Whether it's that old handbag, the shirt that doesn't fit, the pencil that needs sharpening, the dishwasher that needs emptying, the car that needs repairing, the friend who keeps calling round, you know in your heart which needs your attention and which needs to be dropped.

Try to get rid of anything that isn't on track with your current task or long-term goal and you'll find it's like getting rid of a sandbag around your ankles.

Once you've removed the things which aren't part of your current task, you'll have physical and mental space to move forward.

There won't be anything in your line of vision, or anything underfoot, or anything beeping, to cause a distraction...

...and if there is, at least you'll know it's been your choice for it to be there and that you've decided it's making a positive contribution towards your goal.

Know when you work best

Everyone has a different time when they are at their peak when working.

When do you work best?

> Rachael says: "I prefer working in the morning and early afternoon. I try not to take client calls after 4pm as that's the time I reserve for my partner, family and friends."

Are you someone who works late into the night? If so, you may not be ready to start work again first thing in the morning.

Or maybe your best hours are like Rachael's, making an early start and finishing the day while it's still light outside.

When is your peak time?

Make a note over the next week of your hours and put a star when you're feeling at your best performance.

Once you know your peak performance time you can arrange your day, restructuring where possible, to give yourself the best chance of achieving your tasks at the optimum time.

Look at all the regular achievements you need to focus on and you can decide what time of the day or night you could be achieving them.

Rework your plans so the things you need the most concentration for (the things that drain your energy the most, that you procrastinate on or that you are least sure about), you complete in your peak hours.

See how you feel and also how much more you have achieved, simply by working hardest in your best hours.

Work hard in your best hours.

Reflect on your achievements weekly

It's all too easy to move on from task to task without stopping for a moment to reflect on your achievements.

Start by asking yourself these two questions:

➢ What have I achieved today?

➢ What difference has it made?

At the end of the day, write down 3 things you have achieved. By the end of the week, you'll have 21 things written down and the achievements can be as big or as small as you like. Each achievement is valid.

Rachael says: "It can be hard to give ourselves a pat on the back or blow our own trumpet. I work with clients, teaching them how to recognise their contributions and their achievements."

Recognising what we have achieved in comparison with focussing on what we haven't done, sets us up in a positive mindset.

This positive mindset generates an unstoppable feeling of *"Wow! I've achieved a lot! What more can I get done today?"* and that spurs us on to get the next task started.

Try it!

Write down 3 things you've achieved today:

1. _____

2. _____

3. _____

They can be big achievements or small steps towards your goal. Each item on your list is an accomplishment.

Focus on what has gone well today.

Listen to good things people are saying

As we get older, we don't seem to focus as much on what we've achieved. We stop celebrating small wins.

Why?

Each achievement is still an achievement, no matter how many times you do it, no matter how many people watched or heard about it.

Somewhere between childhood triumphs of putting on a pair of socks by ourselves, riding a bike for the first time, learning a song, or anything you can remember, we stop and new achievements aren't as shiny anymore.

Is it because there's no grown up to show off to? Is it because we worry what people will think?

Maybe it's because we let life take over.

Celebrate your wins!

Every time we celebrate a win, no matter how small that win may seem, we give ourselves a hit of dopamine which is strongly associated with pleasure and reward.

So, next time someone pays you a compliment, you get a round of applause or a standing ovation, enjoy the moment!

You deserve the success. Let people praise your achievements and you'll get a double-hit of dopamine.

➢ Listen to the good things people say about you.

➢ What good things can you say to other people?

Allow yourself to be recognised for the work you've done. It's OK to accept praise and recognition for the time you've spent on tasks for yourself and for others.

Enjoy the success, you've earned it.

Collaborate

You know those things you just never quite get to do?

- ➤ 3 litres of water you aim to drink each day?
- ➤ 30 mins of yoga you aimed for 5 times a week?
- ➤ 1 hour of quality time with your family per day?

Or on a work level, the 10 sales calls you wanted to make today, the 3 invoices you need to send out, the hour on working "on" your business you wanted to do.

Having a trusted and reliable accountability partner can help you achieve all of these things. Accountability partners can be useful for making life choices as well as business strategy and decisions.

Rachael says: "Don't ask your best friend to be your accountability partner - Why? They'll let you off with excuses, an accountability partner won't!"

It's up to you whether you check in with your accountability partner every day, each week, month, or on a quarterly basis.

You might schedule a call or online meeting more regularly if you're organising an event.

You might arrange to chat once a month if you know you'll get distracted and you want someone to check in with you to make sure you've invoiced all your clients.

If there are one-off tasks you don't seem to be getting around to doing, or if you can't think of anyone suitable in your social or work network, you can always buy in accountability hours with companies or individuals who offer this specific accountability service.

Accountability is a sure way of getting things done.

If you can't or won't do it off your own back for yourself, just having someone nudge you from time to time can help you get off the starting blocks, chat at a midway point, and celebrate with you at the end.

Know Your Strengths

If you know your specific strengths and offer your help out to others, you're sure to receive support from others in the areas you need help in return.

We're all good at something.

Just take a minute to think about your strengths.

What are the best things you can think of to say about yourself?

If it helps, write down the first 3 things you think of:

1. _____

2. _____

3. _____

If you're stuck, these are a few ideas to get going:

> ➢ You're organised and good at planning.
>
> ➢ You're always on time.
>
> ➢ You remember birthdays/anniversaries.
>
> ➢ You're kind, thoughtful and conscientious.
>
> ➢ You're good at solving IT problems.
>
> ➢ You make great cakes.
>
> ➢ Your accountancy/bookkeeping qualifications
>
> ➢ You drive a car/ride a bike.

Think back to writing your CV. Maybe you listed your top skills and strengths there. Your list doesn't have to be complete as we're all evolving.

So, with your list of strengths in mind:

> ➢ Who do you know that you could help?
>
> ➢ What do you need help with?
>
> ➢ Who has the strengths you're missing?

What goes around comes back around (not always giving to and receiving from the same person).

You'll get back what you give out and the more you give the more you'll get.

In terms of time management, finding someone with a strength you're missing will have tremendous rewards.

> ➢ Do you hate cold-calling? Find someone who loves it (they'll do it faster and better).
> ➢ Do you struggle with accounts, invoicing and debt collection? Find someone who excels at this.

The more time you save by not doing the things that take you longer than someone else, will free up your time to concentrate on the things you do well.

Maybe you'll see an opportunity to do the same thing for someone else too. Maybe it's something you can charge for, barter with, or give away. It's up to you.

Bonus Tip! Ask Someone For Help

It's ok to ask for help with almost anything and the more you ask for help, the more you'll realise most people like helping people.

Think about it, did you feel good when someone asked you for your expertise, your knowledge, your skills or your help?

You were able to offer something they couldn't do themselves.

Also, the more you ask for help, the more you'll realise that other people are, have been, or will be, in your situation.

They'll have an idea of what you're going through and can offer advice or support to help you. They might share their experiences or reassure you it will all be OK.

There's always someone around.

➤ Ask your family for advice.

➤ Ask your friends for recipe ideas.

➤ Ask your contacts who they know that does what you need doing.

Rachael says: "I've recently started a new business and I needed to practice my presentation, so I messaged some friends and asked if they would be willing to help. In the space of 30 minutes I'd booked 4 brand new appointments and delivered my first presentation to one of my networking friends."

Jenny says: "My Grandma was a firm believer in the right thing being available at the right time. She had stories you'd never expect to turn out how they did, just from asking someone for help and offering help to those in need."

Acknowledgements

We would like to thank a few people for inspiring us to write this book and supporting us on our journey:

4NetworkingOnline

Without 4Networking, Jenny and Rachael might never have met! Living 285 miles apart we met face to face when Jenny made the round trip to visit the northern 4Networking face to face meetings.

https://4nonline.biz

Steve Westrop

Another connection through 4Networking, Steve has helped both Jenny and Rachael to build, maintain and boost their online presence to get the attention they deserved: he keeps IT simple, helping you shine online.

https://s6connect.com

Jonathan Smythe

A truly creative genius, whom Rachael and Jenny met through 4Networking. On mentioning this book, Jon said, "I love helping friends out, please can I do your cover FOC" and we agreed!

https://www.smooothdesgins.co.uk

Adrian Cuthill and Dominic Fenton

Another chance meeting through 4Networking led to creating Dragonball Sports Ltd. Developing the game from Jenny's books into a real-world sport, yet again proves achieving a work/life balance is possible.

https://www.dragonball.uk.com

If you'd like to find out more about what Rachael does or to book a 1-to-1 or Power Hour with her, visit:

http://getfocus.guru

If you'd like to find out more about what Jenny does with copywriting and children's books, please visit:

https://www.sammyrambles.co.uk

Future Books:

Rachael and Jenny are already talking about the next in the series of Focus Guru books. We are really looking forward to working together to create our new book which will be released soon.

https://getfocus.guru

Printed in Great Britain
by Amazon

32070088R00079